SPECTACULAR
SPACE TRIVIA

By Laura Shereda

Gareth Stevens
Publishing

Please visit our website, www.garethstevens.com. For a free color catalog of all our high-quality books, call toll free 1-800-542-2595 or fax 1-877-542-2596.

Library of Congress Cataloging-in-Publication Data

Shereda, Laura.
 Spectacular space trivia / Laura Shereda.
     p. cm. — (Ultimate trivia challenge)
 Includes bibliographical references and index.
 ISBN 978-1-4339-8297-2 (pbk.)
 ISBN 978-1-4339-8298-9 (6-pack)
 ISBN 978-1-4339-8296-5 (library binding)
 1. Astronomy–Miscellanea–Juvenile literature. I. Title.
 QB46.S445 2014
 520—dc23

                                        2012047238

First Edition

Published in 2014 by
Gareth Stevens Publishing
111 East 14th Street, Suite 349
New York, NY 10003

Copyright © 2014 Gareth Stevens Publishing

Designer: Andrea Davison-Bartolotta
Editor: Greg Roza

Photo credits: Cover, p. 1 (satellite) Photodisc/Thinkstock, (stars) Konstantin Mironov/Shutterstock.com, (Jupiter) courtesy of NASA/Damian Peach; pp. 4, 5, 10 (main), 19, 20, 23, 25 (both), 26 (nails), 29 iStockphoto/Thinkstock; p. 6 courtesy of NASA; p. 7 (top) Keystone-France/Gamma-Keystone via Getty Images; p. 7 (bottom) Space Frontiers/Getty Images; p. 8 NASA/Newsmakers/Getty Images; p. 9 SSPL/Getty Images; p. 10 (inset) Triff/Shutterstock.com; p. 11 Siegfried Layda/Photographer's Choice/Getty Images; p. 12 (Neptune) NASA/JPL/Science Source/Getty Images; p. 12 (Venus) Digital Vision/Thinkstock; p. 13 (inset) Stocktrek Images/Thinkstock; pp. 13 (main), 16, 18 Stocktrek Images/Getty Images; p. 14 Hemera/Thinkstock; p. 15 AbleStock.com/Thinkstock; p. 17 MarcelClemens/Shutterstock.com; p. 21 NASA/Time Life Pictures/Getty Images; p. 22 courtesy of 2MASS/Wikimedia Images; p. 24 Victor Habbick Visions/Science Photo Library/Getty Images; p. 26 (astronaut) NASA/AFP/Getty Images; p. 27 NASA via Getty Images; p. 28 Stockbyte/Thinkstock.

Printed in the United States of America

CPSIA compliance information: Batch #CS13GS: For further information contact Gareth Stevens, New York, New York at 1-800-542-2595.

CONTENTS

Words in the glossary appear in **bold** type the first time they are used in the text.

BLAST OFF!

We live on planet Earth, which is the third planet from the sun in our solar system. The solar system may seem like a big place. However, it's a mere speck of dust compared to outer space as a whole.

The universe is made up mostly of empty space, but it contains many surprises. Scientists called astronomers are hard at work exploring space, searching for the answers to the universe's many mysteries. Let's blast off and learn some amazing facts about outer space!

our solar system

"Universe" comes from a Latin word that means "the whole" or "the whole world." Another word for the universe is "cosmos," which comes from a Greek word that means "order" or "world."

EXPLORING SPACE

What was the first man-made satellite to orbit Earth?

On October 4, 1957, the Soviet Union (Russia) launched *Sputnik 1*—the first man-made **satellite** to **orbit**

Sputnik 1 **replica**

Earth. It circled the planet about 1,400 times. The following year, the Soviets launched *Sputnik 2*, which carried a dog named Laika into space.

BONUS TRIVIA »» BONUS TRIVIA
BONUS TRIVIA »» BONUS TRIVIA
BONUS TRIVIA
BONUS TRIVIA »» BONUS TRIVIA
BONUS TRIVIA »» BONUS TRIVIA

By April 2012, there were nearly 1,000 artificial satellites orbiting Earth. About 440 of them were US satellites.

Who was the first woman in space?

In 1963, Valentina Tereshkova—a Russian astronaut—became the first women in space. She orbited Earth 48 times before landing safely. Since then, many women astronauts have been in space. Sally Ride became the first American woman in space in 1983.

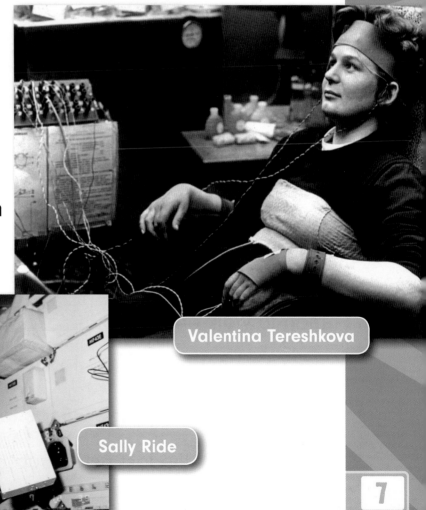

Valentina Tereshkova

Sally Ride

Because there is no wind or weather on the moon, astronauts' footprints will stay there forever.

How many men have walked on the moon?

In 1969, American Neil Armstrong became the first man to walk on the moon, followed soon after by fellow astronaut Buzz Aldrin. By 1972, 10 more men, all Americans, had walked on the moon. Eugene Cernan and Harrison Schmidt were the last astronauts to do this.

What are the only man-made objects to travel outside the solar system?

In 1977, NASA launched two **space probes**—*Voyager 1* and *Voyager 2*. Their mission was to explore Jupiter and Saturn, but they've since traveled beyond the outermost reaches of our solar system. These probes continue to send **data** to scientists back on Earth.

BONUS TRIVIA

Voyager 1 is so far away from Earth it takes more than 17 hours for data sent by the probe to reach scientists at NASA.

SUN AND MOON

How old is the sun?

Long ago, our solar system was a giant cloud of gas and dust. Around 4.6 billion years ago, the cloud began to **collapse** toward the center. Then, about 4.5 billion years ago, our sun finished forming at the center of this cloud. The planets and their moons followed soon after.

Our sun is middle-aged. Scientists believe it will last for another 5 billion years.

The moon moves 1.6 inches (4 cm) away from Earth every year. Many years from now, it will appear smaller in the sky and will be too far away to create a total solar eclipse.

If the sun is so much larger than the moon, why are total solar eclipses possible?

During a total **solar** eclipse, the moon moves in front of the sun, completely blocking it out. The sun is 400 times bigger than the moon. However, it's also 400 times farther away from Earth than the moon. This **coincidence** makes them appear the same size from Earth.

THE PLANETS

What are the hottest and coldest planets in the solar system?

The temperature on Venus is around 860° Fahrenheit (460°C), day and night, no matter where you are on the planet. Neptune is about 2.8 billion miles (4.5 billion km) from the sun. The temperature there dips to −322° Fahrenheit (−197°C).

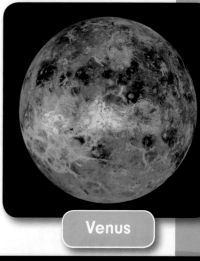

Venus

Neptune

BONUS TRIVIA

Why is Venus hotter than Mercury? Mercury might be closer to the sun, but Venus is surrounded by heavy clouds, which trap heat.

Olympus Mons is a volcano. It was formed when hot, liquid rock poured out of Mars and cooled to form a mountain.

Where is the biggest mountain in the solar system?

Olympus Mons is a giant mountain on Mars. In fact, it's the biggest mountain in the solar system! It's about 340 miles (550 km) across. It's about 16 miles (25 km) tall, which is about three times taller than Earth's tallest mountain, Mount Everest.

Why would your weight be different if you could visit another planet?

Gravity is the force that pulls objects toward the center of a planet. It's what gives us weight. The greater a planet's mass, the stronger its gravity. You'd be heavier on a planet that has more mass than Earth. You'd be lighter on a planet that has less mass than Earth.

planet	times Earth's gravity	100 pounds on Earth is...
Mercury	0.38	38 pounds
Venus	0.9	90 pounds
Earth	1	100 pounds
Mars	0.38	38 pounds
Jupiter	2.36	236 pounds
Saturn	0.92	92 pounds
Uranus	0.89	89 pounds
Neptune	1.13	113 pounds

This chart shows how much 100 pounds on Earth would weigh on other planets. How much would you weigh on other planets?

Saturn is made mostly of gases. Scientists believe it has a small, rocky core.

BONUS TRIVIA

Saturn glows! It gives off more light than it receives from the sun, and no one is sure why yet.

Which planet would float if you could drop it in water?

Density is a measure of the matter in a given volume. Saturn has the lowest density of any planet in the solar system. That means its matter isn't packed together very tightly. In fact, Saturn is less dense than water. That means it would float in a giant ocean!

POOR PLUTO!

If Pluto was once a planet, why isn't it a planet anymore?

In 2006, many scientists agreed that Pluto could no longer be called a planet because it hasn't "cleared the neighborhood" around its orbit. In other words, Pluto shares its orbital space with other space objects, mainly comets. Because of this, Pluto is now called a dwarf planet.

Pluto

Eris

Scientists have discovered many other dwarf planets beyond Neptune. This includes Eris, which many scientists believe is actually larger than Pluto.

COMETS AND ASTEROIDS

Where do comets come from?

Comets are small space objects made of ice and dust left over from when the solar system first formed. They come from an area beyond Neptune called the Kuiper Belt, which is where Pluto is found. Others come from even farther out, from a region called the Oort Cloud.

Comets are sometimes called "dirty snowballs."

BONUS TRIVIA

As a comet gets closer to the sun, energy from the sun blows ice and dust away from the comet, forming a "tail."

What is the largest known asteroid?

Ceres is an asteroid about the size of Texas. It orbits the sun between Mars and Jupiter along with thousands of other asteroids in the asteroid belt. It makes up about one-third of the mass of the asteroid belt. Ceres is so big it's now considered a dwarf planet.

THE MILKY WAY

How many stars are in the Milky Way galaxy?

A galaxy is an enormous system of stars and planets held together by gravity. It's similar to a solar system in that the planets and stars orbit the center. We live in the Milky Way galaxy. Scientists **estimate** that our galaxy contains about 200 billion stars!

STARS AND LIGHT

What is the fastest thing in the universe?

Light is really, really fast—faster than any other thing in the universe. Light travels about 186,000 miles (300,000 km) a second. That's about 700 million miles (1.127 billion km) an hour. At this speed, sunlight takes an average of 8 minutes and 20 seconds to reach Earth.

How long does it take the sun's light to reach Neptune?

Neptune is the planet farthest from the center of our solar system. The blue gas giant is an average of 2.8 billion miles (4.5 billion km) from the sun. It takes just over 4 hours for the sun's light to reach the distant planet.

What star is nearest to Earth?

That's easy—the sun! The sun is an average of 93 million miles (149.7 million km) away from Earth. The next closest star is Proxima Centauri. It's about 25 trillion miles (40 trillion km) away! It takes about 4.2 years for light from Proxima Centauri to reach Earth.

Proxima Centauri is a red dwarf star. It is smaller and cooler than the sun.

When we see stars that are a billion light-years away, we're seeing how they looked a billion years ago. Many of those stars have already died out!

How far away are the most distant stars?

The stars are unbelievably far away, so far that scientists measure cosmic distances in light-years. One light-year is the distance light travels in 1 year, or 5.8 trillion miles (9.3 trillion km). The most distant stars discovered so far are about 13 billion light-years away!

BLACK HOLES

Why are black holes black?

A black hole forms when a superheavy star collapses on itself because its gravity is so powerful. All the star's matter squeezes together in a very small space. The gravity is so strong that nothing—not even light—can escape. This is why they're called "black holes."

Scientists know black holes exist, even though they can't see them, because their gravity affects nearby space objects.

How far away is the black hole that's nearest to Earth?

Scientists once thought a black hole at the center of the Milky Way was the closest one to Earth. However, in 1999, scientists discovered a closer black hole, which is "just" 1,600 light-years away. Scientists first noticed it because they observed it "stealing" gases from a nearby star.

The black hole—named V4641 Sgr—is near a large star in the Sagittarius constellation.

FUN STUFF ABOUT SPACE!

What is "cold welding," and what does it have to do with outer space?

Welding is a process of joining two pieces of metal with heat. However, it's possible to join pieces of some metals in a **vacuum** without heat. This is called cold welding. Cold welding is possible in space because there's no air there.

BONUS TRIVIA

The air around Earth reacts with metal and gives it a natural coating (think about rust). If this coating isn't allowed to form—as in a vacuum—cold welding is possible.

Why doesn't sound travel in space?

We hear sounds because sound waves cause **molecules** in the air to move very quickly, or vibrate. However, there are no, or very few, molecules in outer space. This means there's nothing to carry sound waves. You've probably seen movies where there are sounds in space, but they're wrong!

How much junk is orbiting Earth?

The US Space **Surveillance** Network tracks more than 8,000 objects orbiting Earth. This includes more than 2,500 satellites, some of which work, and some that are dead. The rest is "space junk" that includes rocket parts, nuts, bolts, and pieces of plastic.

There are millions more pieces of space junk orbiting Earth that are too small to track, such as paint chips from spacecrafts.

Scratch the Surface

Now you've learned some pretty far-out trivia about outer space. However, space is very big, and there's much more to learn. Which planet travels the fastest? Which one has the shortest day? Are there other planets like Earth out there? Keep exploring space to find the answers to these and many other questions.

GLOSSARY

coincidence: the occurring of two events that happen at the same time by chance but seem to be connected

collapse: to fall down or cave in

data: facts and figures

estimate: to make a careful guess about an answer based on the known facts

launch: to send out with great force

molecule: a very small piece of matter

orbit: to travel in a circle or oval around something, or the path used to make that trip

satellite: an object that circles Earth in order to collect and send information or aid in communication

solar: having to do with the sun

space probe: an unmanned spaceship sent to study objects in the solar system

surveillance: the act of watching someone or something closely

vacuum: an empty space without any matter in it

FOR MORE INFORMATION

Books

Bingham, Caroline. *First Space Encyclopedia*. New York, NY: DK Publishing, 2008.

National Geographic. *Ultimate Weird but True*. Washington, DC: National Geographic, 2011.

Prinja, Raman. *Spacecraft and the Journey into Space*. Mankato, MN: QEB Publishing, 2013.

Websites

Our Solar System
www.kidsastronomy.com/solar_system.htm
Learn much more about our solar system.

Voyager: The Interstellar Mission
voyager.jpl.nasa.gov
Learn everything there is to know about the *Voyager* probes, including where they are right now.

INDEX